~A Special Gift~

For:

Bessie

From:

Pat

Date:

_10-12-99_

Original Artwork © 1998 Debbie Mumm

Text © 1998 The Brownlow Corporation
6309 Airport Freeway
Fort Worth, Texas 76117

ISBN: 1-57051-097-0

Printed in China.

TEA TIME FRIENDS

Text by Caroline Brownlow
Illustrated by Debbie Mumm

Brownlow

Other Miniature Books

A NOTE FROM DEBBIE

Sharing our hearts and a cup of tea
with friends is always a special time.

Why not call a friend and plan
to have tea this very week!
Whether at home or in your
favorite tearoom, make some time
and make some memories together.

Love, Debbie

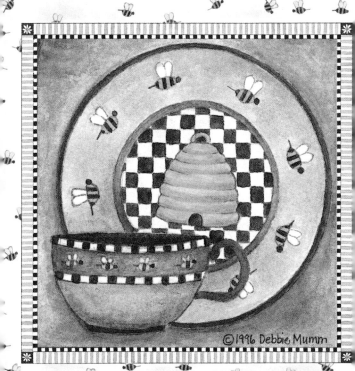

©1996 Debbie Mumm

A SWEET FRIENDSHIP

If I live by the human equivalents of grace,
love, forgiveness and faith with
those who occupy space in my life,
thinking more of belonging than of owning,
seeking to maintain the relationship
as a matter of supreme importance,
those relationships will never grow "stale,"
but sweeter every day.

~SANDRA W. HOOVER~

BEARING BURDENS

Never to judge rashly; never
to interpret the actions of others
in an ill-sense, but to compassion~
ate their infirmities, bear their
burdens, excuse their weaknesses,
and make up for their defects~
to hate their imperfections,
but love themselves, this is
the true spirit of charity.

~ NICHOLAS CAUSSIN ~

To have a friend is to have one of the
sweetest gifts that life can bring; to be a
friend is to have a solemn and tender
education of soul from day to day.

~ AMY ROBERTSON BROWN ~

Never refuse a healthy portion of love
or honey. Both are basic necessities
for nourishing the heart and the body.

~ CAROLINE BROWNLOW ~

In a world where everyone seems
to be larger and louder than yourself,
it is very comforting to have a small,
quiet companion.

~PETER GRAY~

Remember the teakettle:
when it's up to its neck
in hot water, it sings.

~EARLY AMERICAN FOLK WISDOM~

PROVERBS OF FRIENDSHIP

A friend hears the song in my heart and
sings it to me when my memory fails.

No people feel closer or more friendly
than those who are on the same diet.

We fall down by ourselves,
but it takes a friendly hand to lift us up.

I do not concern myself with great matters
or things too wonderful for me.
But I have stilled and quieted my soul.

~ PSALM 131:1 ~

Nostalgia is remembering the pleasures
of our old kitchen when we were kids,
without remembering how long it took
to wash the dishes.

~ CAROLINE BROWNLOW ~

A Blessed Thing

A blessed thing it is for any man or woman to have a friend; one human soul whom we can trust utterly; who knows the best and the worst of us, and who loves us in spite of all our faults; who will speak the honest truth to us, while the world flatters us to our face, and laughs at us behind our back; who will give us counsel and reproof in the day of prosperity and self-conceit; but who, again, will comfort and encourage us in the day of difficulty and sorrow, when the world leaves us alone to fight our own battle as we can.

~Kingsley~

HONEY TEA

Honey is a wonderful,
all-natural sweetener
for a delicious cup of tea.
Instead of sugar,
put a teaspoon or two
of honey in your tea and stir.
Yum!

HONEY GINGERBREAD

1½ cups sifted flour ~ ¼ cup sugar

2 teaspoons baking powder

¼ teaspoon baking soda

½ teaspoon salt

½ teaspoon ginger ~ ½ teaspoon cloves

½ teaspoon cinnamon

1 egg, well beaten ~ ½ cup honey

½ cup milk or water

4 tablespoons melted shortening

Sift dry ingredients together three times.
Mix egg, honey, milk and shortening.
Combine liquid and dry ingredients
and beat thoroughly.
Pour into greased pan and bake
in moderate oven
(350° F) 30 to 35 minutes.
Makes one (8" x 8") cake ~ or 12 muffins.

BACK DOOR
FRIENDS

Back door
friends are the
ones who come
in when the
whole world
goes out.

WELCOME

© Debbie Mumm

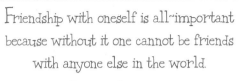

Friendship with oneself is all~important
because without it one cannot be friends
with anyone else in the world.

~ELEANOR ROOSEVELT~

While there's tea, there's hope.

~SIR ARTHUR PINERO~

The fingers of God touch your life
when you touch a friend.

~MARY DAWN HUGHES~

Teddy bears are constant, loving,
adoring friends. They let you eat
all the frosting from the cake.

LITTLE CUPS OF TEA

Little cakes, little tarts,
Little cups of tea:
Just enough for my dear friends,
And just enough for me.

~CAROLINE BROWNLOW~

Oh! yet
Stands the church clock at ten to three?
And is there honey still for tea?

~RUPERT BROOKE~

They serve God well,
who serve his creatures.

~CAROLINE SHERIDAN NORTON~

To avoid old age,
keep taking on new thoughts
and throwing off old habits.

~PROVERB~

Was anything real ever gained
without sacrifice of some kind?

~ARTHUR HELPS~

It is easier to catch flies
with honey than with vinegar.

~ENGLISH PROVERB~

The busy bee teaches two lessons:
one is not to be idle, and the other
is not to get stung.

~EARLY AMERICAN PROVERB~

Friends help us to mend
our broken hearts.

~ANTIQUE SAMPLER~

THE MIRACLE OF FRIENDSHIP

Is there any miracle on earth
to compare with that of discovering
a new friend, or having that
friend discover you? So much is at
stake, but I will gladly risk
everything to give a
promising relationship
a chance.

~ALEX NOBLE~

Hunny

A Fragile Thing

Since human life is a fragile and
unstable thing, we have no choice
but to be ever on the search for
people whom we may love,
and by whom we may be loved in
turn, for if charity and
goodwill are removed
from life, all the joy
is gone out of it.

~ CICERO ~

TIME FOR TEA

©1996 Debbie Mumm

TEARS AND LAUGHTER

At my table, sit with me
I'll pour coffee or some tea;
Perhaps we'll share our tears and laughter,
And be friends forever after.

Friendship is like two clocks
keeping time.

~ANONYMOUS~

Life is the flower of which
love is the honey.

~AMERICAN PROVERB~

Therefore, encourage one another
and build each other up, just as in fact
you are already doing.

~1 THESSALONIANS 5:11~

Kindness is the sunshine
in which virtue grows.

~ANONYMOUS~

JUST THE SAME

If apples were pears, and peaches were plums,
And the rose had a different name,~
If tigers were bears, and fingers were thumbs,
I'd love you just the same.

In shining old shoes or old silver,
it don't make no difference what
brand of polish you uses.
You has got to mix elbow grease
with it to make it shine.

~EARLY AMERICAN FOLK WISDOM~

ICED TEA

In 1904, "iced tea" was invented at the St. Louis World's Fair when an extreme heat wave caused patrons to forsake their custom- ary cup of tea. In desperation, tea vendors added ice and offered it as a summer cooler. The rest, as they say, is history.

Many a heart learns to love
from its first teddy bear.

~ A. K. ~

I've had my trials and troubles.
The Lord has given me both vinegar
and honey, but he has given me the vinegar
with a teaspoon and the honey with a ladle.

~ BILLY BRAY ~

The cup of tea on arrival at
a country house is a thing which,
as a rule, I particularly enjoy.

~ P. G. WODEHOUSE ~

If you add a word a day to your
vocabulary, at the end of the year your friends
will wonder who you think you are.

~ ANONYMOUS ~

MAMAW'S HONEY BARS

3/4 cup oil ~ 1/4 cup honey

1 egg ~ 1 cup sugar

2 cups flour, sifted

1 teaspoon soda

1/2 teaspoon salt

1 1/2 teaspoons cinnamon

1 cup chopped pecans

1 teaspoon vanilla

In one bowl, mix the oil, honey,
egg, and sugar together.
In another bowl, mix the flour,
soda, salt, and cinnamon together.
Mix the contents of the two bowls together.
Stir in the pecans and vanilla.
Spread on a large jelly roll pan
that has "sides."
Bake at 350° for 20 minutes.
Cut into bars, about 1" x 2 ½".

WITH THOSE WE LOVE

To be with those we love is enough.
Ah, how true it is! and it is a
happiness which will outlast this life.
In this thought I love to rest.

~MADAME SWETCHINE~

The comfort of having a
friend may be taken away,
but not that of having had one.

~SENECA~

Friendship is a spiritual thing.

It is independent of matter or space or time.

That which I love in my friend is not

that which I see. What influences me in

my friend is not his body, but his spirit.

~JOHN DRUMMOND~

We cannot live on honey alone.

~JAPANESE PROVERB~

I can live for two months

on a good compliment.

~MARK TWAIN~

LOVE BEARS ALL THINGS

Bear with each other
and forgive each other.

~COLOSSIANS 3:13~

Praise be to the Lord,
to God our Savior,
who daily bears
our burdens.

~PSALM 68:19~

Love bears all things.

~1 CORINTHIANS 13:7~

Be completely humble and gentle;
be patient, bearing with
one another in love.

~EPHESIANS 4:2~

Bear one another's
burdens.

~GALATIANS 6:2~

I'D LIKE TO "BEE"

I'd like to be the sort of friend that
you have been to me.
I'd like to be the help that you've
been always glad to be;
I'd like to mean as much to you
each minute of the day
As you have meant, old friend of mine,
to me along the way.

~EDGAR A. GUEST~

THE TEA BAG

In 1908, New York tea importer
Thomas Sullivan sent out samples
of different kinds of tea, each of which had
been sewn into individual little silk bags.
Some customers mistakenly made tea
with the little packages. Soon
many people were complaining when
the tea was not in the tiny pouches,
and the tea bag was invented.

THE WITNESS OF THE BEE

We talked of the beauty of the world
of God and the great mystery of it.
Every blade of grass, every insect, ant,
and golden bee, all so amazingly know their
path, though they have not intelligence,
they bear witness to the mystery of God
and continually accomplish it themselves.

~ FYODOR DOSTOYEVSKI ~

Have nothing in your homes
that you do not know to be useful
and believe to be beautiful.

~WILLIAM MORRIS~
World Renowned Designer

The noblest service comes
from unseen hands,
And the best servant
does his work unseen

~OLIVER WENDELL HOLMES~

THERE IS HONEY YET

You say that this world to you
seems drained of its sweets!
I don't know what you call sweet.
Honey and the honeycomb,
roses and violets, are yet in the earth.
The sun and moon yet reign in heaven,
and the stars keep up their pretty twinklings.
Meats and drinks, sweet sights and sweet smells,

a country walk, spring and autumn,
follies and repentance, quarrels and
reconcilements have all a sweetness by turns.
Good humor and good nature,
friends at home that love you,
and friends abroad that miss you~
you possess all these things, and more
innumerable, and these are all sweet things.
You may extract honey from everything.

~CHARLES LAMB~

A clay pot sitting in the sun
will always be a clay pot.
It has to go through the white heat
of the furnace to become porcelain.

~MILDRED WITTE STOUVEN~

Salt your food with humor,
pepper it with wit and sprinkle
over it the charm of fellowship.
Never poison it with the cares of life.

~EARLY AMERICAN FOLK WISDOM~

The one who knows how to show
and to accept kindness will be a friend
better than any possession.

~SOPHOCLES~

Peace to you.
The friends here send their greetings.
Greet the friends there by name.

~3 JOHN 14~

Teddy bears are just about the only toy
that can lose just about everything and
still maintain their dignity and worth.

~SAMANTHA ARMSTRONG~

© Debbie Mumm

As Simple As Honey

We ought to do good to others as simply
and as naturally as a horse runs, or a
bee makes honey, or a vine bears grapes
season after season without thinking
of the grapes it has borne.

~Marcus Aurelius~

I have decided to stick with love.
Hate is too great a burden to bear.

~Martin Luther King, Jr.~

A friend should bear
his friend's infirmities.

~WILLIAM SHAKESPEARE~

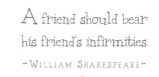

Better to be deprived of food
for three days than of tea for one.

~CHINESE PROVERB~

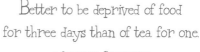

A friend is the gift of God, and He only
who made hearts can unite them.

~ROBERT SOUTHEY~

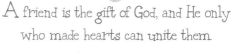

WHAT IS A FRIEND?

A friend is: a push when you've stopped,

a word when you're lonely,

a guide when you're searching,

a smile when you're sad,

a song when you're glad.

A Tribute to Tea

If you are cold, tea will warm you~
If you are heated, it will cool you~
If you are depressed, it will cheer you~
If you are excited, it will calm you.

~William E. Gladstone~
British Prime Minister

ORANGE~HONEY BREAD

2 tablespoons shortening

1 cup honey

1 egg, beaten

1 ½ tablespoons grated orange rind

2 ⅔ cups sifted flour

2 ½ teaspoons baking powder

½ teaspoon baking soda

½ teaspoon salt

¾ cup orange juice

¾ cup chopped pecans

Cream shortening and honey together
thoroughly. Add egg with orange rind.
Sift flour with baking powder, soda, and salt.
Add to creamed mixture alternately
with orange juice. Add nuts.
Bake in greased loaf pan in
325° oven for 70 minutes.
Makes one loaf.

There is a great deal of poetry
and fine sentiment in a chest of tea.

~RALPH WALDO EMERSON~

True friendship is like sound health,
the value of it is seldom known
until it be lost.

~COLTON~

Hunny

©DEBBIE MUMM

HOUSE BLESSING

Bless our home,
Our lives, our friends,
With love, that Lord,
On Thee depends.

~ANTIQUE SAMPLER~